INSTANT MATH
PRACTICE PAGES
FOR HOMEWORK—OR ANYTIME!

by Betsy Franco

SCHOLASTIC
PROFESSIONAL BOOKS

New York • Toronto • London • Auckland • Sydney
Mexico City • New Delhi • Hong Kong • Buenos Aires

For Emily

Cover design by Jim Sarfati

Cover and interior illustrations by Steve Cox

Interior design by Ellen Matlach Hassell
for Boultinghouse & Boultinghouse, Inc.

ISBN: 0-439-37077-9

Contents

Introduction

Looking for a fun way to build and review important math skills? Here are 50 reproducible practice sheets that are flexible and easy to use—kids can complete them at home or in school, independently or in groups. Each practice page features appealing illustrations, topics kids enjoy, and simple instructions so that children can work on their own. Pull out these practice pages for quick activities during the school day, or send them home as skill-building homework assignments.

You'll find several pages on each of the following topics that are coordinated with the NCTM standards:

- Patterns
- Addition
- Subtraction
- Comparing and Ordering
- Place Value
- Graphing
- Time
- Money
- Measurement
- Geometry
- Multiplication and Division
- Fractions

These pages were designed to appeal to second and third graders. The topics relate to their world and interests: pets, storybook characters, favorite foods, messy rooms, and more. In addition, children will enjoy the variety of formats. They'll play a coin-toss game, measure the snake family, go on a shape safari, color fraction flags, and much, much more.

We hope that you and your students enjoy *Instant Math Practice Pages for Homework—or Anytime!* Whether you use them for homework or class work, they are sure to give children's math skills a boost.

How to Use This Book

These practice pages were designed for flexible use. Kids can work on them individually, in pairs, in small groups, or as a whole class. Have students work on the sheets:

- for reinforcement of skills during a unit

- for review after a unit is completed

- when they are finished with other class work

- as a morning activity to start the day

- after lunch to settle back into learning

- as skill-building homework

Refer to the table of contents to locate a practice page that builds a particular math skill. For easy reference, math skills are also listed in a box at the top of each practice page. You can use the pages in the order they are presented or rearrange the order to suit the needs of your class.

Most of the activity pages require only a pencil and eraser. A few require scissors, glue, crayons, and other materials that are easily accessible. If sending home the sheets as homework, review the directions in advance to answer any questions that children have. You might also review the materials and modify them if necessary.

After students have finished a page, have them share and discuss their answers with partners, in groups, or as a class. On pages 63–64, you'll find a complete answer key. Allow students to share and discuss their responses and problem-solving strategies. You might first have them discuss their ideas in small groups so that everyone has a chance to participate. Then review the answers together as a group to be sure that everyone understands how to solve each problem.

Feel free to modify any of the practice pages to fit your students' needs. (For example, on page 18 you could create additional cards with more difficult subtraction problems after your students have mastered the ones presented here.) For an extra challenge, have children think of their own problems based on the problems and information provided on each page—for example, challenge students to think of additional telephone and bike lock patterns on page 8. Have students share the problems they made up so that the rest of the class can solve them.

Name _____

Date _____

Hang Out the Socks

Look at the socks on the clothesline.
Draw socks to continue the patterns.
Then color the socks.

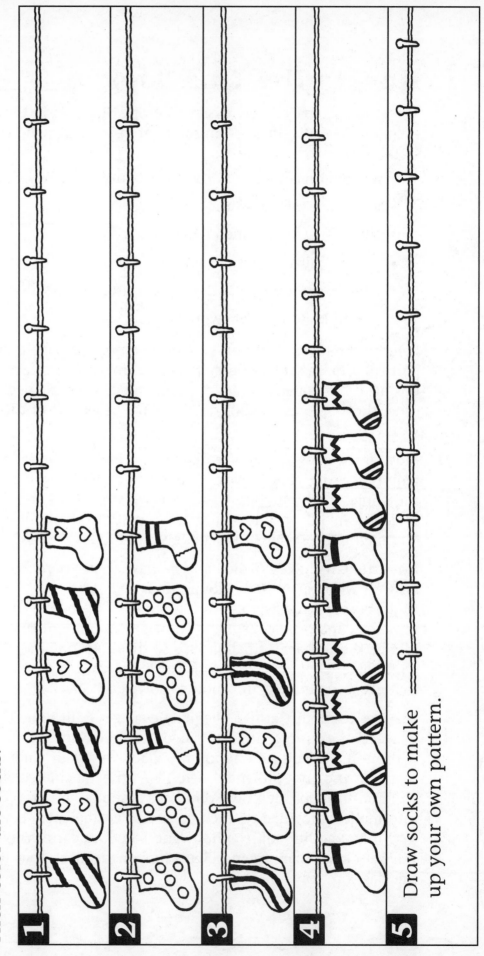

5 Draw socks to make up your own pattern.

Instant Math Practice Pages for Homework—or Anytime!   Scholastic Professional Books

Name _____   Date _____

Cracker Patterns

The shapes below are made from crackers!
Sometimes the shapes in the pattern get bigger.
Sometimes the shapes in the pattern get smaller.
Draw shapes that continue each pattern.

1

_____   _____

2

_____   _____

3

_____   _____

4

_____

5 (Hint: How many sides does each shape have?)

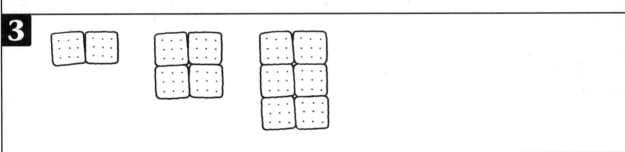

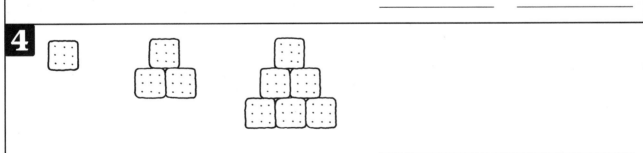

_____

Telephone and Bike Lock Patterns   PATTERNS

Each telephone number has a pattern.
Fill in the missing numbers.
(Hint: Read the numbers out loud.)

1 234-567___   **2** 737-373___

3 987-654___   **4** 102-030___

5 112-211___   **6** 246-246___

7 What is your telephone number? _____

Does it have any patterns? Explain. _____

_____

Each bike lock combination
has a pattern.
What is the next number
in each pattern?

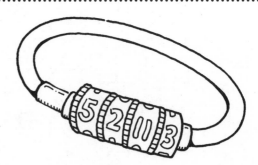

1 2-4-6-_____   **2** 10-20-30-_____

3 1-3-5-_____   **4** 11-22-33-_____

5 5-10-15-_____   **6** 6-8-10-_____

Instant Math Practice Pages for Homework—or Anytime!   Scholastic Professional Books

100 Grid Hunt   PATTERNS

1 Count by twos, starting with **2**. Circle each number
you count. (The first one has been done for you.)

2 Now count by fives, starting with **5**. Mark each number
you count with an X. (The first one has been done for you.)

1	②	3	4	✗5	6	7	8	9	10
11	12	13	14	15	16	17	18	19	20
21	22	23	24	25	26	27	28	29	30
31	32	33	34	35	36	37	38	39	40
41	42	43	44	45	46	47	48	49	50
51	52	53	54	55	56	57	58	59	60
61	62	63	64	65	66	67	68	69	70
71	72	73	74	75	76	77	78	79	80
81	82	83	84	85	86	87	88	89	90
91	92	93	94	95	96	97	98	99	100

3 Write ten numbers that you name
when you count by twos *and* fives.

____ ____ ____ ____ ____ ____ ____ ____ ____ ____

Name _____ Date _____

Leprechaun Math

Color each coin
a different color.

1 Add the numbers on each leprechaun.
   Find the coin that has the sum printed on it.
   Color each leprechaun the same color as its matching coin.

2 Write the numbers from the coins in
   the circles below, from least to greatest.

3 What pattern do you see? _____

_____

10

Butterfly Doubles

Count the dots on each wing and write the number. Then find the sums.

Draw the correct number of dots on each wing. Then find the sums.

1
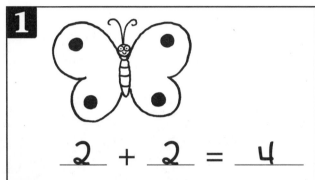

$$\underline{2} + \underline{2} = \underline{4}$$

2
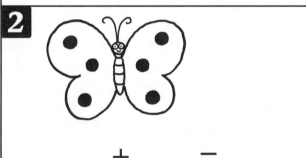

$$\underline{} + \underline{} = \underline{}$$

3
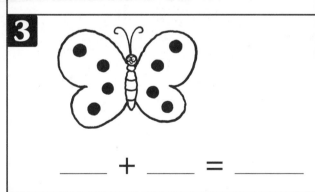

$$\underline{} + \underline{} = \underline{}$$

4
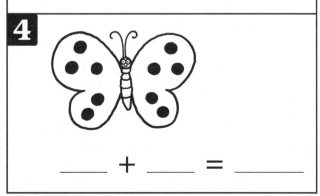

$$\underline{} + \underline{} = \underline{}$$

5

$$7 + 7 = \underline{}$$

6

$$9 + 9 = \underline{}$$

7

$$8 + 8 = \underline{}$$

Instant Math Practice Pages for Homework—or Anytime!   Scholastic Professional Books

Magic Square Lily Pads ADDITION

1

Each frog had a number.
The frogs jumped onto a big log.
If you add the number on each pair of frogs,
the sum should be 10.
Write these numbers on the blank frogs: **2**, **3**, **4**, **5**, **6**, **7**, **8**
The first pair of frogs has been done. 1 + 9 = 10

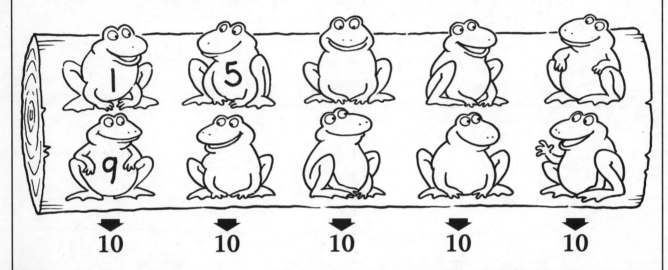

10   10   10   10   10

2

The frogs jumped
onto a giant lily pad.

If you add any row,
column, or diagonal,
the sum is 15.

Write these numbers
on the blank frogs:
1, **2**, **3**, **4**, **7**

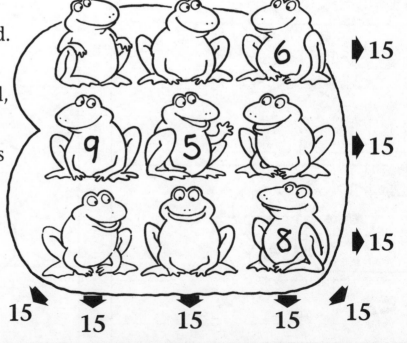

15

15

15

15   15   15   15   15

Instant Math Practice Pages for Homework—or Anytime! Scholastic Professional Books

Name _____ Date _____

Coin-Toss Game

For 2 Players
You need 2 coins or chips and a Coin-Toss Game Board.

To Play:
Player 1 gently tosses both coins onto the game board, one at a time. The score is the sum of the numbers on which the coins land. Player 1 writes the score in the chart.

If a coin lands on a line or does not land on the game board, add a zero.

Player 2 takes a turn in the same way.

Compare the two scores and circle the higher number. The player with the higher score wins the round.

Round	Player 1	Player 2
1		
2		
3		
4		
5		
6		
7		

Instant Math Practice Pages for Homework—or Anytime! Scholastic Professional Books

13

Coin-Toss Game Board ADDITION

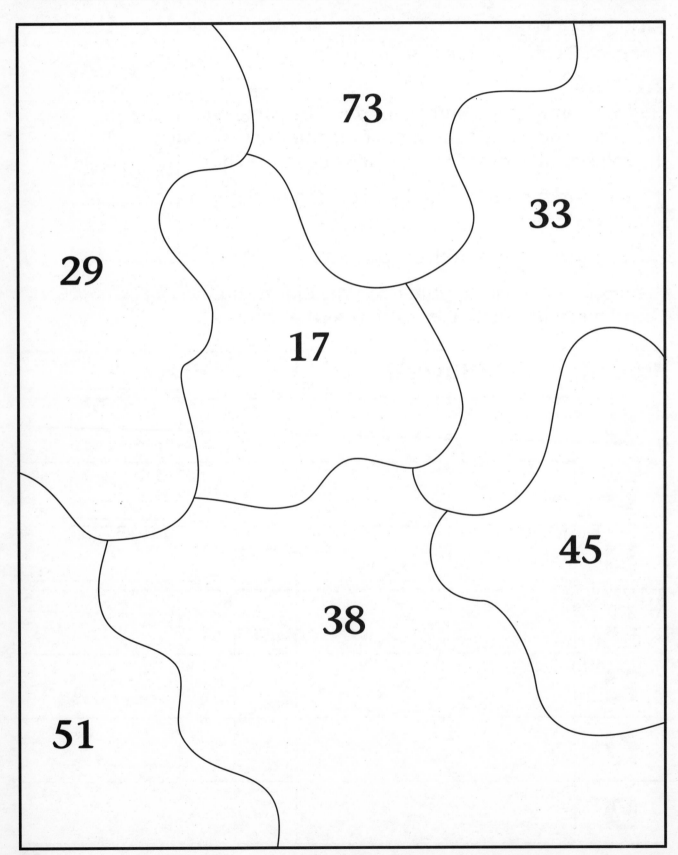

73

33

29

17

45

51

38

Instant Math Practice Pages for Homework—or Anytime! Scholastic Professional Books

Target Number

ADDITION

Circle two numbers to get the target number as a sum.
You should circle one number in each row.

1

12	13
6	9

Target: 21

2

15	16
3	4

Target: 20

3

14	15
6	9

Target: 21

4

18	16
7	6

Target: 24

5

5	7
16	13

Target: 23

6

8	7
18	15

Target: 25

BONUS

Circle three numbers that add up to the target number.

7	4
6	5
16	17

Target: 25

Name _____   Date _____

Subtraction Bikes

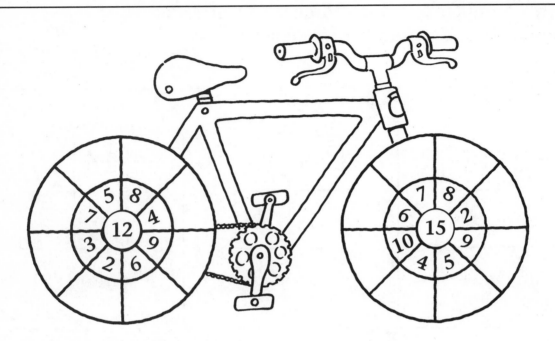

Subtract each number
on the wheel from 12.

Subtract each number
on the wheel from 15.

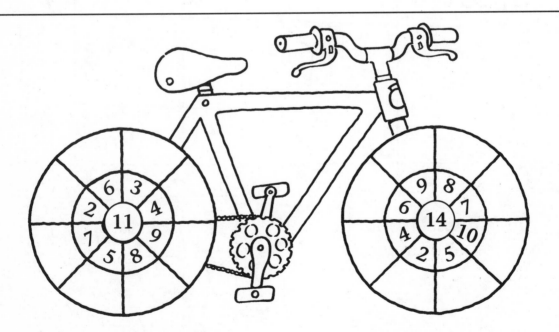

Subtract each number
on the wheel from 11.

Subtract each number
on the wheel from 14.

Instant Math Practice Pages for Homework—or Anytime!   Scholastic Professional Books

Racetrack

You will need someone to time you (in seconds) as you race around the track.

To Play:

Cut out the Racetrack Cards on page 18. Place ten of the cards facedown in the spaces on the track.

When the timer says "Go!" turn over the cards one by one and say the answer to each problem.

Go around the track again.
Can you break your record?

Then try again with ten different cards.

Name _____ Date _____

Racetrack Cards **SUBTRACTION**

Cut out the cards along the solid lines.

10 − 5	9 − 2	8 − 3	15 − 8	7 − 4	12 − 5	13 − 6
8 − 2	14 − 5	9 − 6	18 − 9	12 − 6	16 − 8	11 − 7
17 − 8	7 − 5	10 − 3	15 − 6	9 − 5	12 − 8	11 − 4
6 − 4	11 − 6	12 − 3	9 − 4	15 − 7	14 − 7	13 − 8
12 − 7	13 − 5	16 − 8	19 − 9	9 − 3	8 − 5	17 − 9
11 − 3	14 − 8	9 − 4	10 − 1	12 − 4	15 − 8	16 − 9

18

Instant Math Practice Pages for Homework—or Anytime! Scholastic Professional Books

Name _____   Date _____

What's the Question? SUBTRACTION

Write a question for each problem.
Then answer the question.

1

$$\begin{array}{r} 16 \\ -\ 7 \\ \hline \end{array}$$

Azmi picked 16 apples.

Seven were wormy.

How many were **not wormy**?

Answer _____

2

$$\begin{array}{r} 12 \\ -\ 5 \\ \hline \end{array}$$

Tina had 12 mice.

Five were big.

How many were _____?

Answer _____

3

$$\begin{array}{r} 15 \\ -\ 8 \\ \hline \end{array}$$

Chandra had 15 marbles.

Eight _____ .

How many _____?

Answer _____

4

$$\begin{array}{r} 13 \\ -\ 4 \\ \hline \end{array}$$

Carlos had 13 fish.

_____ .

_____?

Answer _____

5

$$\begin{array}{r} 14 \\ -\ 7 \\ \hline \end{array}$$

Natalie had 14 stickers.

_____ .

_____?

Answer _____

6

$$\begin{array}{r} 18 \\ -\ 9 \\ \hline \end{array}$$

Josh's quilt had 18 squares.

_____ .

_____?

Answer _____

Name _____ Date _____

Subtraction Puzzles   SUBTRACTION

Use these numbers in the problems below: **4, 3, 2, 1**

1

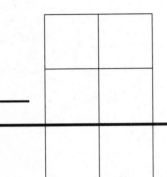

Write a subtraction problem with the largest possible answer.

2

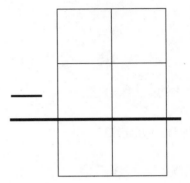

Write a subtraction problem with the smallest possible answer.

Use these numbers in the problems below: **9, 8, 7, 6**

3

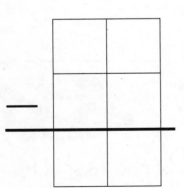

Write a subtraction problem with the largest possible answer.

4

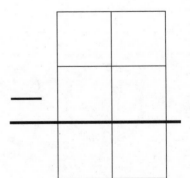

Write a subtraction problem with the smallest possible answer.

Instant Math Practice Pages for Homework—or Anytime! Scholastic Professional Books

You're the Teacher

SUBTRACTION

Morgan did his homework while watching TV, listening to the radio, and playing video games.

Circle his five mistakes and correct them.

Name **Morgan** _____

1. 42
    − 37
    ——
     5

2. 54
    − 26
    ——
    25

3. 60
    − 45
    ——
    15

4. 88
    − 69
    ——
    19

5. 141
    − 73
    ——
    78

6. 93
    − 26
    ——
    68

7. 40
    − 24
    ——
    28

8. 87
    − 78
    ——
     9

9. 152
    − 65
    ——
    77

Instant Math Practice Pages for Homework—or Anytime!   Scholastic Professional Books

21

Name _____   Date _____

Fairy Tale Names

Count the letters in each name. Then write the number of letters.

Name	Number of Letters
Big Bad Wolf	
Little Red Riding Hood	
Rumpelstiltskin	
Cinderella	
Rapunzel	
Rip Van Winkle	
Prince Charming	
Little Red Hen	
_____ (your full name)	

Now compare the names. Use <, >, or =.

EXAMPLE: Snow White has 9 letters. Sleeping Beauty has 14 letters.

Snow White < Sleeping Beauty

1. _____ > _____

2. _____ < _____

3. _____ = _____

4. _____ > _____

5. _____ < _____

6. _____ = _____

Instant Math Practice Pages for Homework—or Anytime! Scholastic Professional Books

Name _____ Date _____

Telephone Book Math

Use the telephone book.

1 Look up your last name. _____

Do more than 20 people or less than 20 people have the same last name? _____

2 Look up the last name of one of your friends. _____

Do more than 20 people or less than 20 people have the same last name? _____

3 Look up the last name **Blake**.

Do more than 20 people or less than 20 people have the same last name? _____

4 Look up another last name. _____

Do more than 20 people or less than 20 people have the same last name? _____

5 Now look up another last name. _____

Do more than 20 people or less than 20 people have the same last name? _____

6 Think of a name that you think more than 20 people have. _____

Look it up. Were you right? _____

Name _____ Date _____

Newspaper Hunt

You will need an old newspaper or magazine to cut up.
Look through the newspaper or magazine for the numbers below.
Cut out the numbers and glue them in the appropriate boxes.

1 Find a number between 5 and 10.

2 Find a number less than 50.

3 Find a number between 30 and 40.

4 Find a price less than $15.

5 Find a number greater than 100.

6 Find a number that is greater than 60 and less than 80.

7 Find a number greater than 300.

Instant Math Practice Pages for Homework—or Anytime! Scholastic Professional Books

Name _____ Date _____

How Long Is That Book? COMPARING & ORDERING

Each of the books below is opened to the last two pages.
Write the number of the last page of each.
Then compare each pair of books.
Circle the book with more pages.

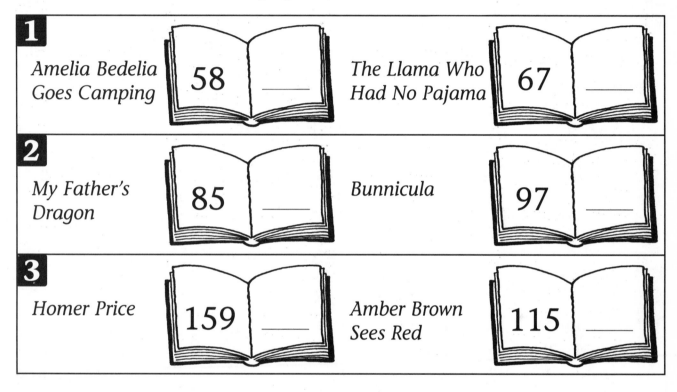

1

Amelia Bedelia Goes Camping | 58 ____ | The Llama Who Had No Pajama | 67 ____

2

My Father's Dragon | 85 ____ | Bunnicula | 97 ____

3

Homer Price | 159 ____ | Amber Brown Sees Red | 115 ____

Now find books in your home, classroom, or library.
Write the title and the last two page numbers of each.
Circle the book in each pair with more pages.

4 Title: _____ Title: _____

5 Title: _____ Title: _____

Name _____ Date _____

Have Fun With Ten!   PLACE VALUE

Ten bats live in each cave.
Some bats have flown out of each one.
Tell how many bats are still inside each cave.

1 _____ bats

2 _____ bats

3 _____ bats

4 _____ bats

5 Circle sums of 10. Find two or three numbers that connect horizontally, vertically, or diagonally. The numbers should add up to 10.

2	5	9	5	3	2
7	2	5	4	8	6
4	4	2	2	5	7
6	5	7	1	2	3
2	9	1	3	4	5
3	7	6	7	4	9

6 Write all the ways to add two numbers to make 10.

0 + 10 = 10

___ + ___ = 10

___ + ___ = 10

___ + ___ = 10

___ + ___ = 10

___ + ___ = 10

___ + ___ = 10

___ + ___ = 10

___ + ___ = 10

___ + ___ = 10

___ + ___ = 10

7 Use three numbers to make 10.

___ + ___ + ___ = 10

___ + ___ + ___ = 10

Instant Math Practice Pages for Homework—or Anytime! Scholastic Professional Books

Number Search

Look for two-digit numbers in old magazines or newspapers.
Cut out the numbers. Then glue or tape them into the boxes below.
Tell how many tens and how many ones are in each number.

17		
_1_ tens _7_ ones	___ tens ___ ones	___ tens ___ ones
___ tens ___ ones	___ tens ___ ones	___ tens ___ ones

Now look for three-digit numbers.
Cut them out and glue them in the boxes below.
Tell how many hundreds, tens, and ones are in each number.

570	
_5_ hundreds _7_ tens _0_ ones	___ hundreds ___ tens ___ ones
___ hundreds ___ tens ___ ones	___ hundreds ___ tens ___ ones

Name _____ Date _____

Number Scramble PLACE VALUE

1 Write as many three-digit numbers as you can.
Use these numbers: **3**, **5**, **7**
Use each number once in each number you make.

___ ___ ___   ___ ___ ___   ___ ___ ___

___ ___ ___   ___ ___ ___   ___ ___ ___

2 Which is the smallest number you made?

_____

3 Which is the largest number you made?

_____

BONUS Write the largest number in hundreds, tens, and ones.
EXAMPLE: 264 = 200 + 60 + 2

_____ = _____ + _____ + _____

4 Write as many three-digit numbers as you can.
Use these numbers: **4**, **6**, **8**
Use each number once in each number you make.

___ ___ ___   ___ ___ ___   ___ ___ ___

___ ___ ___   ___ ___ ___   ___ ___ ___

5 Which is the smallest number you made?

_____

6 Which is the largest number you made?

_____

BONUS Write the largest number in hundreds, tens, and ones.

_____ = _____ + _____ + _____

Name _____ Date _____

Favorite Foods

Leslie took a poll of her classmates to find out their favorite foods. She made a tally mark for each person's response.

Fill in the graph with the information from Leslie's poll.

pizza	ЖН
fruit	IIII
cereal	II
hot dog	III
cookies	ЖН II

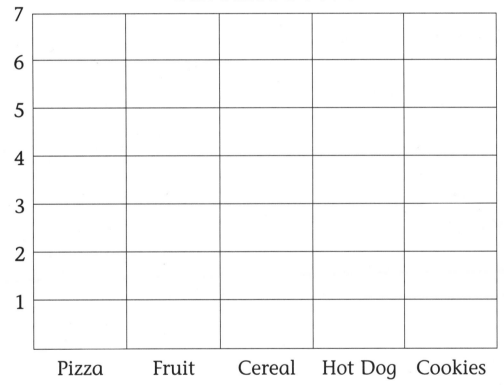

Favorite Foods

7
6
5
4
3
2
1

Pizza   Fruit   Cereal   Hot Dog   Cookies

1 Do more people like pizza or fruit? _____

How many more? _____

2 How many more people chose hot dogs than cereal? _____

3 Which food got the most votes? _____

4 Which food got the least votes? _____

Family Members

GRAPHING

Beth and Mark made a graph of the number of people in their families. Fill in the graph to show how many family members Kenny and Se-Yun have each.

Kenny has 3 family members.   Se-Yun has 6 family members.

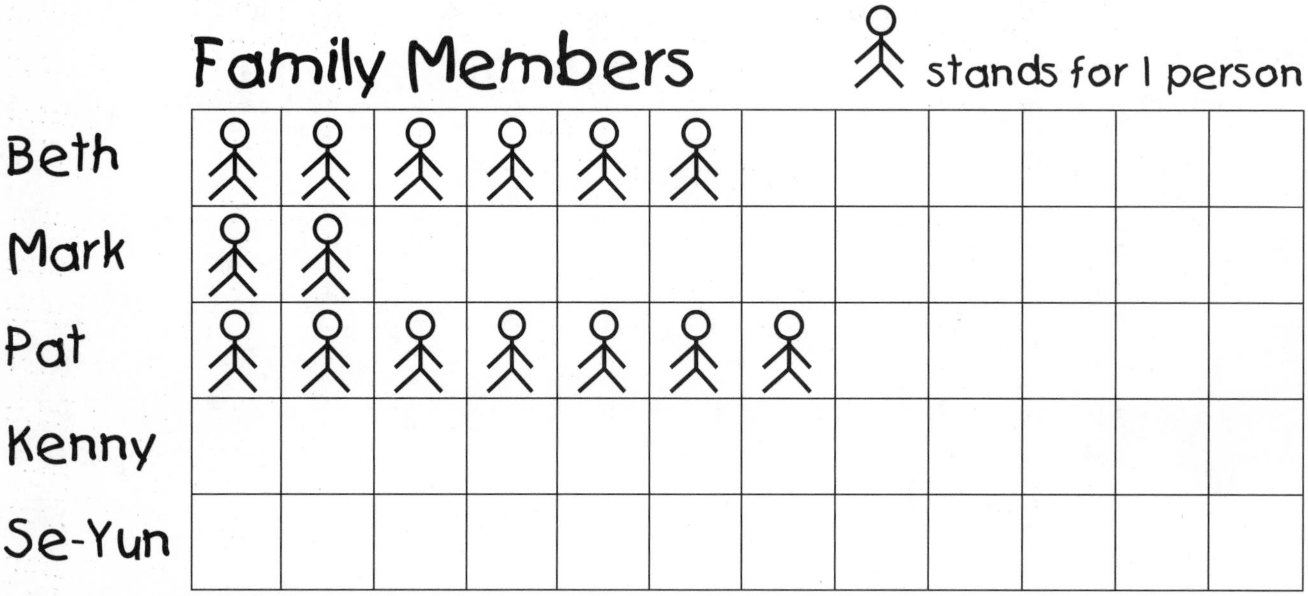

Family Members

⚥ stands for 1 person

Beth	⚥	⚥	⚥	⚥	⚥	⚥						
Mark	⚥	⚥										
Pat	⚥	⚥	⚥	⚥	⚥	⚥	⚥					
Kenny												
Se-Yun												

Fill in the blanks.

1 How many more family members does Pat have than Beth? _____

2 How many more family members does Pat have than Kenny? _____

3 Who has more family members, Mark or Pat? _____

4 Who has more family members, Se-Yun or Pat? _____

5 Who has more family members, Mark or Se-Yun? _____

How many more? _____

6 Who have the same number of people in their families?

_____ and _____

Instant Math Practice Pages for Homework—or Anytime! Scholastic Professional Books

Graphing Carla's Room GRAPHING

1 Look at the drawing of Carla's room on page 34.

Count each picture, sock, and book. Circle or color each object as you count. Tell how many of each object there are in all.

Kind of Object	How Many in All?
pictures	
socks	
books	

2 Now make a graph. Fill in the correct number of boxes for each kind of object. Then answer the questions below.

3 There are more

_____ than

_____ .

How many more? _____

4 There are more

_____ than

_____ .

How many more? _____

Things in Carla's Room

	pictures	socks	books
15			
14			
13			
12			
11			
10			
9			
8			
7			
6			
5			
4			
3			
2			
1			

Graphing Carla's Room GRAPHING

Name _____ Date _____

34

Instant Math Practice Pages for Homework—or Anytime!   Scholastic Professional Books

Concentration Time

Play this game of Concentration with another person.
Cut out the cards and shuffle them.
Place the cards facedown in three rows of six.

To Play:

Player 1 turns over any two cards and reads the time on each.
- If the two times match, the player keeps the cards and takes another turn.
- If the times don't match, the player turns the cards facedown. Player 2 then takes a turn.

The player with more cards wins.

Instant Math Practice Pages for Homework—or Anytime!   Scholastic Professional Books

35

Find the Mystery Day `TIME`

Jeff's class picked a day for their pizza party.
The students will take a school bus to the pizza parlor.
They chose a day that had no other special events.
Use the clues to figure out which day they picked.
Cross out the days they didn't pick.
Circle the day they picked.

Clues

1. They can't have the party on the weekends.

2. On Thursdays the class goes to the library.

3. The school buses are not available on Mondays and Wednesdays.

4. They are going on a field trip on the second Tuesday of the month.

5. A guest is coming on the first and third Fridays.

6. There is an assembly on the last Tuesday.

7. The third Tuesday is a school holiday.

8. They can't go the first week of March.

9. On the 12th and 26th, the pizza parlor already has a party.

MARCH						
Sunday	Monday	Tuesday	Wednesday	Thursday	Friday	Saturday
	1	2	3	4	5	6
7	8	9	10	11	12	13
14	15	16	17	18	19	20
21	22	23	24	25	26	27
28	29	30	31			

Instant Math Practice Pages for Homework—or Anytime! Scholastic Professional Books

Have a Good Time

TIME

Fill in the blanks.

1 6:50 A.M. is ___50___ minutes after ___6:00 A.M.___.

2 2:30 P.M. is _____ minutes before _____.

3 1:20 P.M. is _____ minutes after _____.

4 9:45 P.M. is _____ minutes before _____.

Draw hands to show these times.

5 1 hour past 4:00 P.M.

6 1 hour before 5:30 A.M.

7 2 hours past 10:35 A.M.

8 2 hours before 2:15 P.M.

Draw hands on the clocks to show the times you usually do these activities. Write the times on the lines.

9 Wake up

10 Go to bed

11 Have lunch

12 Have dinner

Name _____   Date _____

Are These Animals Late? `TIME`

Each of these animals has somewhere to go.
Look at the time each animal needs to arrive.
Then look at the clock.
Is the animal late?

1   Party at 4:00 P.M.

What time is it? _____ P.M.

Is Rabbit late? _____

2   School starts at 8:30 A.M.

What time is it? _____ A.M.

Is Mouse late? _____

3   Flute lesson at 3:25 P.M.

What time is it? _____ P.M.

Is Hen late? _____

4   Art class at 10:00 A.M.

What time is it? _____ A.M.

Is Frog late? _____

38

Instant Math Practice Pages for Homework—or Anytime!   Scholastic Professional Books

Pairs of Piggy Banks

Look at each pair of piggy banks.
Write the amount of money in each one.

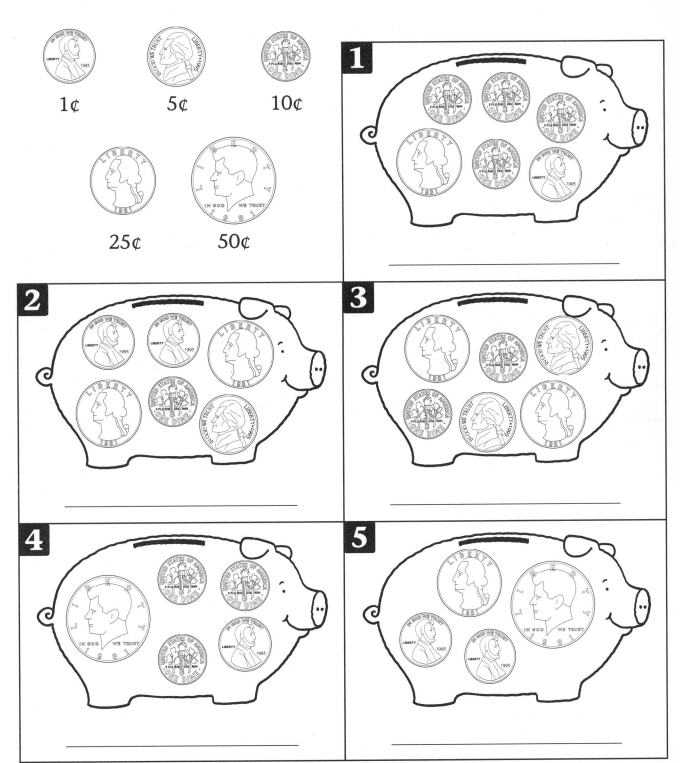

1¢ 5¢ 10¢

25¢ 50¢

1 _____

2 _____

3 _____

4 _____

5 _____

Name _____ Date _____

Squirrels Go Shopping   MONEY

Winter's coming!
Stock up on nuts!

acorns
4¢ each

peanuts
5¢ each

walnuts
6¢ each

almonds
7¢ each

pecans
8¢ each

cashews
9¢ each

1 Sarah Squirrel bought two different nuts for 13¢.
Which two nuts could she have bought?

_____   _____

Write an addition sentence to show how you know:

_____ ¢ + _____ ¢ = _____

2 Sammy Squirrel bought two different nuts for 17¢.
Which two nuts could he have bought?

_____   _____

Write an addition sentence to show how you know:

_____ ¢ + _____ ¢ = _____

3 Sandy Squirrel bought two different nuts for 15¢.
Which two nuts could she have bought?

_____   _____

Write an addition sentence to show how you know:

_____ ¢ + _____ ¢ = _____

40

Instant Math Practice Pages for Homework—or Anytime! Scholastic Professional Books

Name _____   Date _____

Coin Guessing Game

Write the values
of the coins.

____ ____ ____ ____

1

Mike has 3 coins.
They are worth 31¢.
What coins does Mike have?
Write the value of each coin.

_25¢_ _____ _____

2

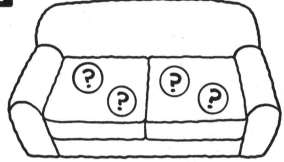

Tanya found 4 coins in
the couch.
They are worth 70¢.
What coins did Tanya find?

____ ____ ____ ____

3

Lily has 4 coins in her piggy
bank. She has 25¢.
What coins are in Lily's
piggy bank?

_____ _____ _____ _____

4

José has 5 coins in his pocket.
He has 46¢.
What coins are in his pocket?

____ ____ ____ ____ ____

Pet Sale

How much is
in your pocket?

_____

fish
$1.39

hamster
$3.50

bunny
$4.25

bird
$1.19

mouse
$2.39

First estimate if you have enough money to buy the following pets.
Then add the prices to check your estimate.

1

Estimate: Could you buy a bunny and a fish? _____

Then add: How much would they cost all together? _____

2

Estimate: Could you buy a hamster and a bird? _____

Then add: How much would they cost all together? _____

3

Estimate: Could you buy a mouse and a hamster? _____

Then add: How much would they cost all together? _____

4

Estimate: Could you buy a bird and a fish? _____

Then add: How much would they cost all together? _____

Instant Math Practice Pages for Homework—or Anytime! Scholastic Professional Books

Name _____   Date _____

How Long?

Find each of these things in your classroom or at home. Measure each one to the nearest inch. If you need a ruler, cut out the one at the bottom of the page.

1 a pencil

about _____ inches

2 a book

about _____ inches

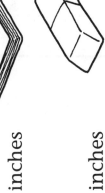

3 an eraser

about _____ inches

4 your shoe

about _____ inches

5 your hand

about _____ inches

Now choose five other objects to measure.

1 _____

about _____ inches

2 _____

about _____ inches

3 _____

about _____ inches

4 _____

about _____ inches

5 _____

about _____ inches

inches | 1 | 2 | 3 | 4 | 5 | 6 | 7 | 8 | 9

43

Estimate and Measure MEASUREMENT

1

Estimate which is wider:　**window　door**　(Circle one.)

How wide is a window? Measure in hand spans.

_____ hand spans

How wide is a door? Measure in hand spans.

_____ hand spans

Which is wider? _____

2

Estimate which is longer:　**backpack　chair leg**　(Circle one.)

How long is your backpack? Measure in hand spans.

_____ hand spans

How long is your chair leg? Measure in hand spans.

_____ hand spans

Which is longer? _____

3

Estimate which is longer:　**pencil　pen**　(Circle one.)

Measure your pencil in thumbs.

_____ thumbs

Measure a pen in thumbs.

_____ thumbs

Which is longer? _____

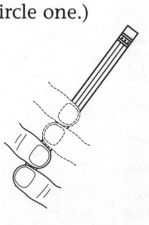

Instant Math Practice Pages for Homework—or Anytime! Scholastic Professional Books

Name _____

Date _____

Measuring the Snake Family

Meet the Snake family!
Measure each snake to the nearest inch and record the length.
If you need a ruler, cut out the one at the bottom of the page.

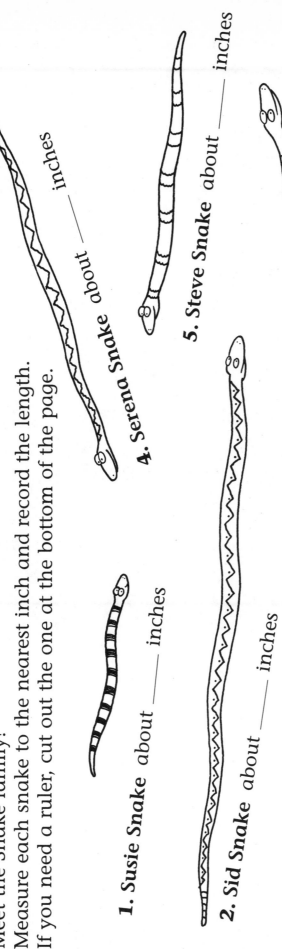

1. Susie Snake about ____ inches

2. Sid Snake about ____ inches

3. Sebastian Snake about ____ inches

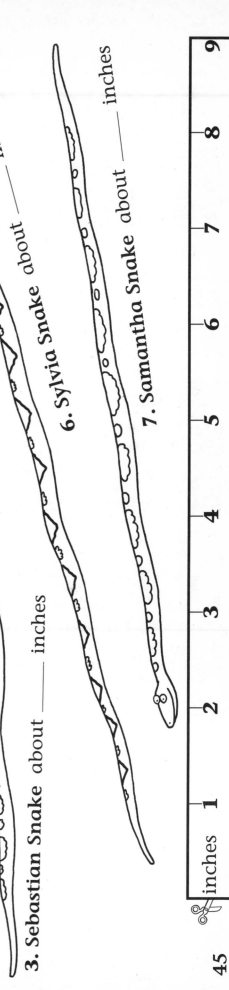

4. Serena Snake about ____ inches

5. Steve Snake about ____ inches

6. Sylvia Snake about ____ inches

7. Samantha Snake about ____ inches

inches 1 2 3 4 5 6 7 8 9

45

Name _____ Date _____

Square or Rectangle? MEASUREMENT

Measure your classroom or a room at home.
Is the room a square or a rectangle?

To find out, use the ruler on page 47 or
measure with footsteps (heel to toe).

☐	☐
Square	Rectangle

1 Measure the front wall in feet (or footsteps).

length: _____

2 Measure the side wall in feet (or footsteps).

length: _____

3 Are the front and side walls the same length? _____

If not, which is longer? _____

4 Is the room a square or a rectangle?
Draw a plan of the room in the correct box.

Square
The walls are almost
the same length.

Rectangle
One wall is longer than the other.

Instant Math Practice Pages for Homework—or Anytime! Scholastic Professional Books

Square or Rectangle?

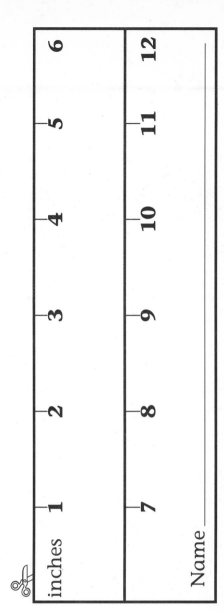

Ruler   Cut apart the strips.
Tape the ends together so that the
numbers are in order from 1 to 12.
Do not overlap the edges.

inches	1	2	3	4	5	6
7	8	9	10	11	12

Name

Square or Rectangle?

Ruler   Cut apart the strips.
Tape the ends together so that the
numbers are in order from 1 to 12.
Do not overlap the edges.

inches	1	2	3	4	5	6
7	8	9	10	11	12

Name

Shape Detective

GEOMETRY

Cut out the boxes on page 49.
Sort them into the three groups below.
Glue or tape them in place, or draw them
if you do not have scissors and glue.

Hint: Some shapes do not fit into a category.

Has 4 corners

Has 3 sides

Has more than 4 sides

Instant Math Practice Pages for Homework—or Anytime! Scholastic Professional Books

Name _____   Date _____

Shape Detective

Write the names of the shapes on the lines.
Cut out the boxes.
Then sort them on page 48.

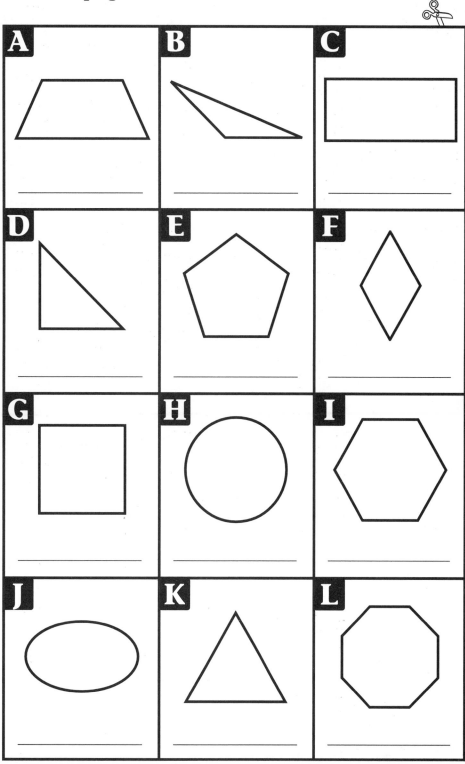

Instant Math Practice Pages for Homework—or Anytime!   Scholastic Professional Books

49

Name _____ Date _____

Dot-to-Dot Shapes

Follow the directions below to draw dot-to-dot shapes.
Connect the dots to make each shape.

1 Draw a square in each box.
Make them different sizes.

EXAMPLE:

 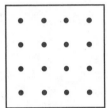 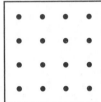 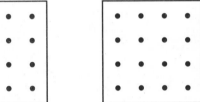

2 Draw a triangle in each box.
Make them different kinds of triangles.

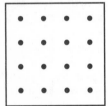 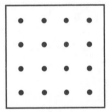 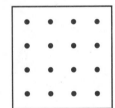 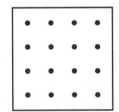

3 Draw a rectangle in each box.
Make them different sizes.

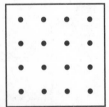 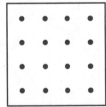 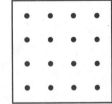 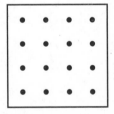

BONUS

Draw an octagon
in the box.
(Hint: It has
8 sides.)

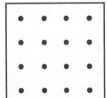

Draw a hexagon
in the box.
(Hint: It has
6 sides.)

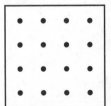

Instant Math Practice Pages for Homework—or Anytime! Scholastic Professional Books

Name _____ Date _____

Shape Safari

Find objects that are different shapes.
Look in your classroom or at home.
Write the objects you find for each shape.
(If you can't find an object for a shape,
think of an object and write it on the lines.)

Find Flat Shapes

1 Rectangle

_____
_____

2 Square

_____
_____

3 Circle

_____
_____

4 Triangle

_____
_____

Find Solid Shapes

5 Cylinder

_____
_____

6 Sphere

_____
_____

7 Cube

_____
_____

8 Rectangular
Solid

_____
_____

Name _____   Date _____

The Bears' Quilt

The bear family made a quilt.
Each bear made a square with 4 red
triangles and 4 yellow triangles.

How can they make each square different?
Color the squares below to show how.

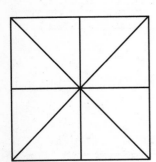
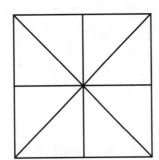

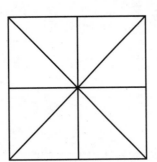
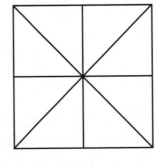
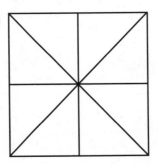
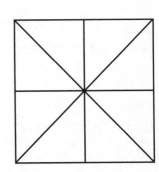

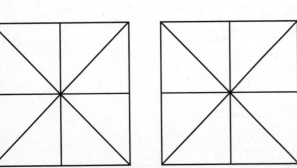
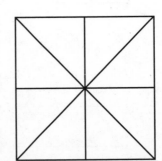
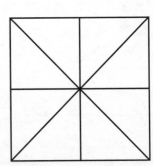

52

Instant Math Practice Pages for Homework—or Anytime!   Scholastic Professional Books

Name _____ Date _____

How Many Legs?

Fill in the blanks.

1 How many legs on

| 1 turkey _____ | 3 turkeys _____ |
| 2 turkeys _____ | 4 turkeys _____ |

2 How many legs on

| 1 cat _____ | 3 cats _____ |
| 2 cats _____ | 4 cats _____ |

3 How many legs on

| 1 ladybug _____ | 3 ladybugs _____ |
| 2 ladybugs _____ | 4 ladybugs _____ |

4 How many legs on

| 1 spider _____ | 3 spiders _____ |
| 2 spiders _____ | 4 spiders _____ |

5 How many legs on

1 squid _____	6 squid _____
2 squid _____	7 squid _____
3 squid _____	8 squid _____
4 squid _____	9 squid _____
5 squid _____	10 squid _____

Name _____   Date _____

Tim's Pet Quilts

MULTIPLICATION & DIVISION

Tim made a quilt for each of his pets.
He used 12 squares for each quilt.
Each quilt was shaped like a rectangle.

Draw quilts on the grid on page 55, one for each pet.
Each quilt should cover the pet from head to tail.
Color the quilts and cut them out.
Then tape them over the animals.

1 snake

2 kitten

3 lizard

5 bunny

4 mouse

54

Instant Math Practice Pages for Homework—or Anytime!   Scholastic Professional Books

Name _____ Date _____

Tim's Pet Quilts

MULTIPLICATION & DIVISION

Instant Math Practice Pages for Homework—or Anytime! Scholastic Professional Books

So Many Mice!

Maria has 12 mice.
Cut out the boxes at the bottom of the page.

1 First she got 2 cages.
Put the same number of
mice in each cage.
(Do not glue them in place.)

How many mice
are in each cage? _____

2 Then Maria decided she
needed 3 cages.
Put the same number of
mice in each cage.

How many mice
are in each cage? _____

3 Finally Maria decided
she needed 4 cages.
Put the same number
of mice in each cage.

How many mice
are in each cage? _____

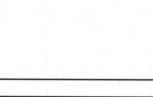

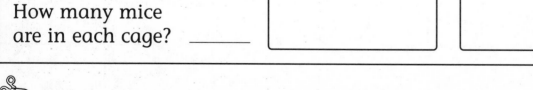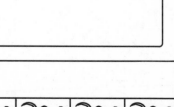

Instant Math Practice Pages for Homework—or Anytime! Scholastic Professional Books

Field Trip Cars

1 Josie's class is going to the teddy bear factory.
Three children will ride in each car.
Draw a circle around the children who will ride in each car.

How many cars do they need? _____

2 Pete's class is going to see the elephant seals.
Five children will ride in each van.
Draw a circle around the children who will ride in each van.

How many vans do they need? _____

3 Rosa's class is going to the Space Museum.
Eight children will ride in each small bus.
Draw a circle around the children who will ride in each bus.

How many small buses do they need? _____

Name _____ Date _____

Fairy Tale Fractions **FRACTIONS**

Shade the fraction shown in each problem.

1 Goldilocks ate $\frac{1}{3}$ of Papa Bear's porridge.	**2** She ate $\frac{2}{3}$ of Mama Bear's porridge.	**3** She ate Baby Bear's whole bowl.

4 Little Red Riding Hood ate $\frac{1}{4}$ of the sandwich in her basket.	**5** Her grandma ate $\frac{3}{4}$ of the sandwich. 

6 Gretel ate $\frac{1}{2}$ of the candy before the witch came. 	**7** Hansel ate $\frac{1}{2}$ of the candy before the witch came. 

8 $\frac{3}{4}$ of the candy on the Gingerbread Man's tummy is green. 	**9** $\frac{1}{4}$ of the candy on his face is red.

10 Hen's chicks ate $\frac{2}{3}$ of the bread she baked. 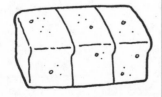	**11** Hen ate $\frac{1}{3}$ of the bread she baked. 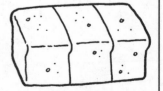

Instant Math Practice Pages for Homework—or Anytime! Scholastic Professional Books

Fractions Bingo

A Game for 2 players

Cut out the cards at the bottom of page 60.

Shuffle the cards and place them facedown in a stack.

Each player needs a bingo game board and 15 chips or other markers.

Write the fractions on the game board before you play.

To Play:

To take a turn, a player picks the top card and reads the fraction.

If a player has that fraction, the player places a marker in that space.

The first player with five markers in a row wins.

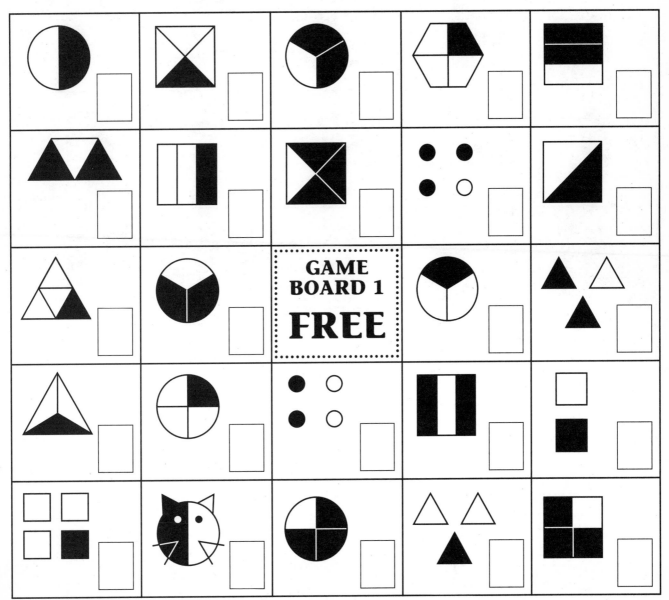

Instant Math Practice Pages for Homework—or Anytime! Scholastic Professional Books

59

Fractions Bingo

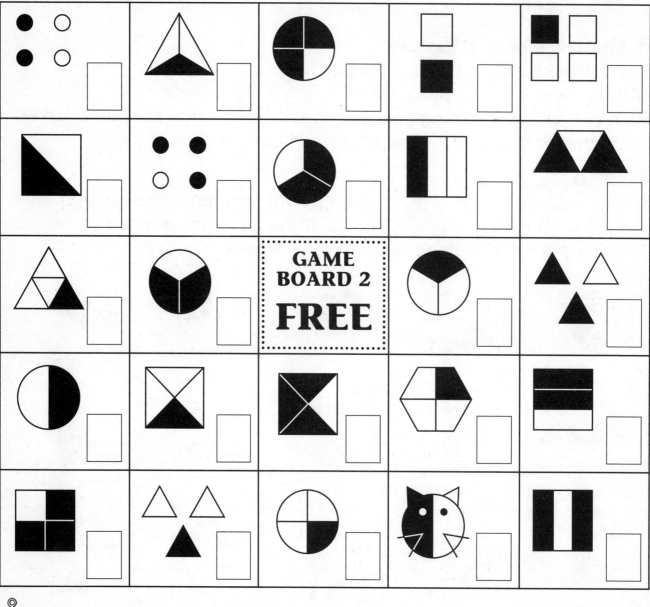

$\dfrac{1}{2}$	$\dfrac{1}{2}$	$\dfrac{1}{2}$	$\dfrac{1}{2}$	$\dfrac{1}{2}$	$\dfrac{1}{3}$	$\dfrac{1}{3}$	$\dfrac{1}{3}$
$\dfrac{1}{4}$	$\dfrac{1}{4}$	$\dfrac{1}{4}$	$\dfrac{1}{4}$	$\dfrac{1}{4}$	$\dfrac{1}{3}$	$\dfrac{3}{4}$	$\dfrac{2}{3}$
$\dfrac{2}{3}$	$\dfrac{2}{3}$	$\dfrac{2}{3}$	$\dfrac{2}{3}$	$\dfrac{2}{3}$	$\dfrac{3}{4}$	$\dfrac{3}{4}$	$\dfrac{3}{4}$

60

Silly Fractions

FRACTIONS

Explain why each of these statements is silly.

1 Bo was seven and a half on his birthday.

_____

_____

_____

2 Theo, Jean, and Fernando split the pie evenly. They each got half of the pie.

_____

_____

_____

3 The quilt had 9 squares.
Half of them were red.

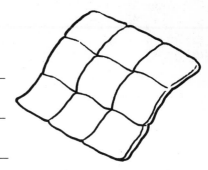

_____

_____

_____

BONUS

Andy had 12 marbles. $\frac{1}{3}$ were red.
$\frac{1}{3}$ were blue. $\frac{1}{3}$ were orange. $\frac{1}{3}$ were yellow.

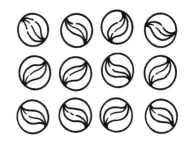

_____

Name _____ Date _____

Class Flags

Bernard's class made several
different flags.
Color the flags below, following
the directions for each.

Which one would you pick
as the class flag?

1 Color $\frac{2}{3}$ red.

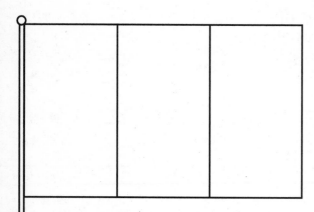

2 Color $\frac{4}{8}$ blue.

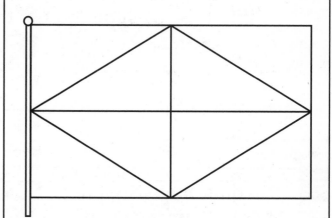

3 Color $\frac{2}{6}$ green.

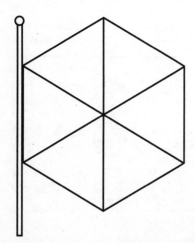

4 Color $\frac{5}{9}$ yellow.

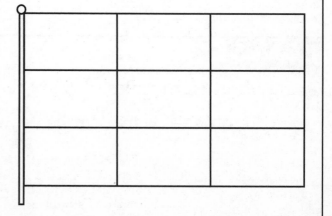

Instant Math Practice Pages for Homework—or Anytime! Scholastic Professional Books

Answer Key

Patterns pp. 6–9

Hang Out the Socks, p. 6
1. striped, hearts, striped, hearts, striped, hearts
2. dots, dots, striped, dots, dots, striped
3. striped, white, hearts, striped, white, hearts
4. striped, striped, zigzag, zigzag, zigzag, zigzag
5. Answers will vary.

Cracker Patterns, p. 7
1.

2.
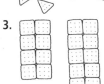
3.

4.

5.

Telephone and Bike Lock Patterns, p. 8
Telephone Numbers
1. 8   2. 7   3. 3
4. 4   5. 2   6. 2
7. Answers will vary.

Bike Lock Combinations
1. 8   2. 40   3. 7
4. 44   5. 20   6. 12

100 Grid Hunt, p. 9
1. All even numbers are circled (numbers in columns 2, 4, 6, 8, and 10).
2. All numbers in columns 5 and 10 are crossed out.
3. 10, 20, 30, 40, 50, 60, 70, 80, 90, 100

Addition pp. 10–15

Leprechaun Math, p. 10
1. 8 + 8 = 16; 4 + 2 = 6;
   7 + 7 = 14; 6 + 4 = 10;
   7 + 5 = 12; 2 + 2 = 4;
   5 + 3 = 8
2. 4, 6, 8, 10, 12, 14, 16
3. The numbers are the even numbers from 4 to 16.

Butterfly Doubles, p. 11
1. 2 + 2 = 4
2. 3 + 3 = 6

3. 4 + 4 = 8
4. 5 + 5 = 10
5. 14, 7 dots on each wing
6. 18, 9 dots on each wing
7. 16, 8 dots on each wing

Magic Square Lily Pads, p. 12
1. 5 + 5 = 10; 3 + 7 = 10;
   4 + 6 = 10; 2 + 8 = 10
2. 2 7 6
    9 5 1
    4 3 8

Coin-Toss Game, pp. 13–14
Game answers will vary.

Target Number, p. 15
1. 12 + 9 = 21
2. 16 + 4 = 20
3. 15 + 6 = 21
4. 18 + 6 = 24
5. 7 + 16 = 23
6. 7 + 18 = 25
BONUS: 4, 5, 16

Subtraction pp. 16–21

Subtraction Bikes, p. 16

Racetrack, pp. 17–18
Students will solve different subtraction problems each time they play the game.

What's the Question? p. 19
1. 9
2. How many were small? 7
3–6. Answers will vary. Possible answers include:
3. Eight were white. How many were black? 7
4. Four were small. How many were big? 9
5. Seven were smiley faces. How many were hearts? 7
6. Nine were black. How many were white? 9

Subtraction Puzzles, p. 20
1. 43 – 12 = 31
2. 31 – 24 = 7
3. 98 – 67 = 31
4. 86 – 79 = 7

You're the Teacher, p. 21
1. correct
2. 54 – 26 = 28
3. correct
4. correct
5. 141 – 73 = 68
6. 93 – 26 = 67
7. 40 – 24 = 16
8. correct
9. 152 – 65 = 87

Comparing & Ordering pp. 22–25

Fairy Tale Names, p. 22
Big Bad Wolf 10
Little Red Riding Hood ... 19
Rumpelstiltskin 15
Cinderella 10
Rapunzel 8
Rip Van Winkle 12
Prince Charming 14
Little Red Hen 12

1–6. Answers will vary. Possible answers include:
1. Little Red Riding Hood > Rapunzel
2. Little Red Hen < Rumpelstiltskin
3. Cinderella = Big Bad Wolf
4. Prince Charming > Rip Van Winkle
5. Cinderella < Little Red Hen
6. Rip Van Winkle = Little Red Hen

Telephone Book Math, p. 23
Answers will vary.

Newspaper Hunt, p. 24
Answers will vary.

How Long Is That Book? p. 25
1. 59; 68 (Circle 68)
2. 86; 98 (Circle 98)
3. 160; 116 (Circle 160)
4–5. Answers will vary.

Place Value pages 26–29

Have Fun With Ten! p. 26
1. 6   2. 8   3. 3   4. 4
5.

2	5	9	5	3	2
3	2	5	4	8	6
4	4	2	2	5	7
6	5	7	1	2	3
2	9	1	3	4	5
3	7	6	7	4	9

6. 1 + 9 = 10; 2 + 8 = 10;
   3 + 7 = 10; 4 + 6 = 10;
   5 + 5 = 10; 6 + 4 = 10;
   7 + 3 = 10; 8 + 2 = 10;
   9 + 1 = 10; 10 + 0 = 10
7. Answers will vary. Possible answers include: 1 + 2 + 7 = 10; 3 + 3 + 4 = 10

Number Search, p. 27
Answers will vary.

Number Scramble, p. 28
1. 375, 357, 537, 573, 735, 753
2. 357
3. 753
BONUS: 753 = 700 + 50 + 3
4. 486, 468, 684, 648, 864, 846
5. 468
6. 864
BONUS: 864 = 800 + 60 + 4

Colorful Fish, p. 29

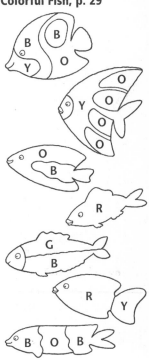

Graphing pp. 30–34

Classroom Pets, p. 30
mammals: hamster, mouse, guinea pig
reptiles and amphibians: gecko, turtle, frog, lizard, snake, salamander
birds: parakeet, finch, parrot
1. 9   2. 9   3. 6
4. <   5. =   6. >

Favorite Foods, p. 31
1. pizza; 1   2. 1
3. cookies   4. cereal

Family Members, p. 32
1. 1   2. 4   3. Pat 4. Pat
5. Se-Yun; 4
6. Beth and Se-Yun

Graphing Carla's Room, pp. 33–34

1. pictures 13 marks 13
   socks 14 marks 14
   (Carla is wearing 2 of them)
   books 11 marks 11
2. pictures 13 boxes
   socks 14 boxes
   books 11 boxes
3. Answers will vary. Possible answers include: There are more socks than pictures. How many more? 1
4. Answers will vary. Possible answers include: There are more pictures than books. How many more? 2

Time pp. 35–38

Concentration Time, p. 35
Game answers will vary.

Find the Mystery Day, p. 36
Tuesday, March 23

Have a Good Time, p. 37
1–4. Answers will vary. Possible answers include:
1. 50, 6:00 A.M.
2. 30, 3:00 P.M.
3. 20, 1:00 P.M.
4. 15, 10:00 P.M.

5.   6.

7.   8.

9–12. Answers will vary.

Are These Animals Late? p. 38
1. 5 P.M.; Rabbit is late.
2. 9 A.M.; Mouse is late.
3. 3 P.M.; Hen is not late.
4. 9:40 A.M.; Frog is not late.

Money pp. 39–42

Pairs of Piggy Banks, p. 39
1. 66¢   2. 67¢   3. 80¢
4. 81¢   5. 77¢

Squirrels Go Shopping, p. 40
1. walnut and almond: 6¢ + 7¢ = 13¢; cashew and acorn: 9¢ + 4¢ = 13¢; pecan and peanut: 8¢ + 5¢ = 13¢
2. pecan and cashew: 8¢ + 9¢ = 17¢
3. cashew and walnut: 9¢ + 6¢ = 15¢; pecan and almond: 8¢ + 7¢ = 15¢

Coin Guessing Game, p. 41
1. 25¢, 5¢, 1¢
2. 25¢, 25¢, 10¢, 10¢
3. 10¢, 5¢, 5¢, 5¢
4. 25¢, 10¢, 5¢, 5¢, 1¢

Pet Sale, p. 42
1. Estimates will vary; $5.64
2. Estimates will vary; $4.69
3. Estimates will vary; $5.89
4. Estimates will vary; $2.58

Measurement pp. 43–47

How Long? p. 43
Answers will vary.

Estimate and Measure, p. 44
Answers will vary.

Measuring the Snake Family, p. 45
1. about 2 inches
2. about 6 inches
3. about 5 inches
4. about 4 inches
5. about 3 inches
6. about 8 inches
7. about 7 inches

Square or Rectangle? pp. 46–47
Answers will vary.

Geometry pp. 48–52

Shape Detective, p. 48
Has 4 corners: A, C, F, G
Has 3 sides: B, D, K
Has more than 4 sides: E, I, L

Shape Detective, p. 49
A. trapezoid   G. square
B. triangle   H. circle
C. rectangle   I. hexagon
D. triangle   J. oval
E. pentagon   K. triangle
F. diamond   L. octagon

Dot-to-Dot Shapes, p. 50
Answers will vary. Possible answers include:

1.
2.
3.

BONUS:

Shape Safari, p. 51
Answers will vary. Possible answers include:
1. door, window
2. bathroom tile, floor tile
3. jar lid, plate
4. pizza slice, cheese slice
5. soup can, tuna can
6. baseball, globe
7. dice, box
8. cereal box, book

The Bears' Quilt, p. 52
Answers will vary. Possible answers include:

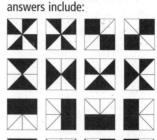

Multiplication & Division pp. 53–57

How Many Legs? p. 53
1. 2, 4, 6, 8
2. 4, 8, 12, 16
3. 6, 12, 18, 24
4. 8, 16, 24, 32
5. 10, 20, 30, 40, 50, 60, 70, 80, 90, 100

Tim's Pet Quilts, pp. 54–55
1. Snake: 1 x 12 squares
2. Kitten: 4 x 3 squares
3. Lizard: 2 x 6 squares
4. Mouse: 2 x 6 squares
5. Bunny : 3 x 4 squares

So Many Mice! p. 56
1. 6   2. 4   3. 3

Field Trip Cars, p. 57
1. 3   2. 3   3. 2

Fractions pp. 58–62

Fairy Tale Fractions, p. 58
1.   2.
3.   4.
5.   6.
7.   8.

9.
10.
11.

Fractions Bingo, pp. 59–60
Game answers will vary.

Silly Fractions, p. 61
1. On your birthday, your age is a whole number.
2. They would each get $\frac{1}{3}$ of the pie.
3. You can't divide 9 squares in half evenly.

BONUS: If $\frac{1}{3}$ are red, $\frac{1}{3}$ are blue, and $\frac{1}{3}$ are orange, there are no marbles left over to be yellow.

Class Fractions, p. 62
Specific shaded sections will vary. Possible answers include:

1. 2 sections shaded

2. 4 sections shaded

3. 2 sections shaded

4. 5 sections shaded